Bully Love

Bully Love

Winner of the 2019 Press 53 Award for Poetry

With love —

[signature]

Patricia Colleen Murphy

Press 53
Winston-Salem

Press 53, LLC
PO Box 30314
Winston-Salem, NC 27130

First Edition

A Tom Lombardo Poetry Selection

Cover Art, "Kakteen Head," Copyright © 2017 by Bedelgeuse,
used by permission of the artist

Cover design by Claire V. Foxx

Author Photo by Nora Kuby

Library of Congress Control Number
2019934225

Printed on acid-free paper
ISBN 978-1-950413-03-4

For John

Acknowledgments

Many thanks to the editors of the publications in which these poems first appeared:

2 Bridges Review, "Eschew"

A Dozen Nothing, "No Coats in October"

Another Chicago Magazine, "Morenci Arizona"

Armchair/Shotgun, "Time to Sheer the Earth's Hair"

Cadillac Cicatrix, "Mia"

Cimarron Review, "Pinetop Lakeside" and "Returning to a Place Known Only in Childhood"

Clackamas Literary Review, "Go Anywhere"

Cutthroat: A Journal of Art and Literature, "Dog-Eared"

Hawaii Review, "Monsoon Season, Tempe Arizona"

Heliotrope, "Salome"

Indiana Review, "Underneath the Tamaracks"

Kalliope, "Ross Township Feed and Tackle"

Mississippi Review, "Good Fences" and "June"

New Orleans Review, "What Good Does a Drop Do"

Nexus, "Wednesday's Path"

Notre Dame Review, "Studious" and "SEER"

Poetry Northwest, "Close to Hermosillo"

Prick of the Spindle, "Dying, Four Ways"

Quarterly West, "The City of Seven Hills"

Seattle Review, "The Implications of Ice"

South Dakota Review, "Three Pound Cutthroat"

Texas Review, "Day Trip: Cave Creek Outfitters"

NewSouth, "Finding a Center"

The South Carolina Review, "Bill Williams Canyon" and "Mid-Street"

Contents

Monsoon Season, Tempe Arizona

The neighbor's poppies
have turned dusty.
The day's end breathes
this, another storm.
Doors slam shut
reminding us
how much we hear
when they are open.
Yesterday was the same,
the house crowned
with the wind's dark tiara.
My father called from Ohio.
He saw the brown
shadow on TV—
forty stories tall,
opaque and rushing.
So this is what it means
to be close to the sky.
What was here is now gone.
This evening we inhale
the dry skin of the desert,
bed down in the belly of the cloud.

Time to Shear the Earth's Hair

Day three and the wind
stopped. Freedom from

slapping branches and mysterious
cranked tapping. From my window

the cows are black and white
candles on a green cake.

Soon I hear a distant mower;
smell the cut grass piling.

Why do I need so badly
to see the thing I hear?

Anticipation is
this crowd of trees between us.

When the tractor starts
I hear the mowing.

When the tractor stops
I hear the mooing.

And so I will live the rest of my life
just short of rapture.

SEER

The house collapsed
its air-conditioned lung.

Waiting for repairs, we rent
a small kitchenette on Apache,

watch the prostitutes clucking back
perfumed and still desperate

for cash or grass. Another August.
My seventh, your tenth. We traded

winter's triplets for summer's twins:
two months of sheer heat, but at least

we are tan, cats splayed on the carpet,
no more greedy lapping. We drive by for

the installation, our street neighborless,
shimmering. Thin repairmen skate

the roof. Crane stationed on the drive.
The hulled compressor hovers over

our books, our bed. Should we
kiss under its mistletoed promise,

our license to live here? Here are
the years approaching like a heat.

Years like a gas, like a living thing.
Unit lowering slow as sand through

a hot sieve, ticking off all this time
we have spent. Consuming more

in the first third of our lives
than most do, ever.

No Coats in October

From here I claim
Ohio is East Coast.

Aunts inquire about
the Sonoran lure.

Not miles of tiled homes,
but creosote, arroyos,

saguaro and alluvial fans.
When my father asks,

do I remember that dry
cleaners off Cheviot Road,

family place. I answer yes.
But it is the same way

I remember him kissing my mother
before her fourth asylum,

like remembering
hayrides on autumn

evenings. Cornfields.
Switchgrass. Cows in mud.

Close to Hermosillo

We are playing a game.
Dim your *blank* for oncoming traffic.
Clean highways are *blank*.

After we make our guesses,
I thumb the thick dictionary
that turns Termina puente

en construcción to *end*
of bridge construction
and ponga la basura en su lugar

to *put trash in its place*.
You are driving again,
which I don't tell you often enough

how much I appreciate.
From our windows windmills
are obedient fan palms.

We watch the landscape
turn riparian. Caution:
road *blank* ahead. No passing

on solid *blank*.
Near the laboratorio we see a girl
with pom poms. A woman in nylons.

A man slumped in a chair.
I want to tell you something,
finally, but we are playing

this game. Don't *blank*
with road signs. Thank you for
choosing *blank*.

Bill Williams Canyon

The station ranger
takes our five-dollar
fee with his hook,
good hand cupping
his camouflage brim,
scratching a scalp itch
with the adjustable
plastic clasp. *February*,
he warns, *ain't no time
to be splashing pants
in that canyon.* He eyes
our Jeep. Knows we'll
go anyway. Parked on
the dam, our first swim
is a mile in, to my armpits,
pack overhead. Weeds
dense, water mild
compared to snow-melt,
bay-freeze back home.
We see no one
except a few deer
poking noses mid-stream.
Sky so blue we might
end up stained.
February. My father
back east is the ice slip,
my mother the chill.

As Overheard in Bars, Backyards

All four lanes of the Beeline are closed, covered
in hay as if all cars long for a place to roost.

My father will pick it up on the news, ask,
Did you hear? Last week he said, *I am*

closer to you than to any other living thing.
Every Friday at 9 a.m. the phone bleats.

First the weather, then what he's reading.
Soon I beg for one of his ten perpetual stories.

Once I got angry with him over an aunt,
slammed the door to prove it, caught

my left fourth finger in the jamb. In the ER
the Days-of-Our-Lives-hot doctor was my age.

Sigma Chi, baby, he said, as he scalpeled off
my fingernail, and, *Would you like to see the pus?*

Then a year of trips to the hand surgeon, his office
filled with photos of his many perfect children.

He asked what I did for a living, nodded, said,
If it doesn't grow back I'll sew a toenail there.

That night I went to a party with two
stunning women. Men crashed like waves.

Don't I know you? and *You come here often?*
The last man smiled at me, *Let's see how I do.*

The only honest try all night. Despite
what my father says, I am not beautiful,

but this man told me a story about saving
a Pointer who almost drowned crossing the Verde.

He took my right hand and said, *So small, so delicate.*
He took my left hand and said, *So how did I do?*

The City of Seven Hills

Imagine last night, cracking blue crabs
at a table in the Sonoran desert.

Even your parents on the Chesapeake
can't catch a trapful. This morning I promise

I will not try so hard. In my dream
I was chugging through fields of wheat.

I saw my aunt's farmhouse, her old Chevrolet.
Inside I sassed her for still living on rented land.

Her cats sashayed past the yard. Her two girls
were my age though I was chunkier,

more clumsy. When we bathed together
the tub squealed, pink with our youth.

This morning I still feel naked. You call your parents,
brag about the price of oysters flown in from the coast.

I stay in our bed a while, feeling heavy, touching
the rise of my belly, my cushion of thigh. This loitering,

you say, is not healthy, but for me it is as important
as last night's lump backfin, boardwalk fries.

It is proof that the succulence lives in me, that I will
never lose the innocence of taste. Here where the land

and everything but me is flat, I need to remember
where I came from—not from the water

or the lack of water, not
from row upon row of chaff.

Barber Shop: Cincinnati, Ohio

At the barber shop the black plastic
comb smooths my father's flattop.
Clippers scrape the nape of his neck.
I sneak snips of hair from his smock,
counting them like hours: every other
Saturday for thirty-two years. I sneak
the years into my hands, counting them
like so many fathers. At the barber shop
my father smiles into the mirror, laughing
about the barber's son-in law: my father
went to school with him, used to drink
with him, got a car stuck on the bank
of the Ohio on New Year's Eve with two
brunettes and him. The white cape billows.
The black snips settle. The barber's hand
and my father's hand meet in a tight union.
I take the barber in one hand, and in the other
hand the father. I lift them high above my head.
Their hands still joined. Nodding, nodding.

Morenci Arizona

The three-ton mine trucks reek
of burning oil and brakes. They rev,

stop to refuel. Today the reservoir
is lapis. The sky is slate but clearing.

The rock is drenched chalk.
Our cuffs rolled nearly to knees.

Our raised voices are tangling
the way I wish our bodies would.

This air is not the only heaviness.
I watch the belts drop chalocite,

malachite, azurite and chrysocolla.
Lion, dragon, hummingbird, sheep:

this way the clouds have meaning.
My only power is this ability to name.

The Implications of Ice

The buckeyes began leaning over the house long
before my mother's madness. From my corner room
I watch their branches in a cold hug, the last
leaves specked with frost, the swaying hard breath
of another fantastic storm. The morning radio

clicks awake with cancellations. The roads are
runways. My father is already out asserting
the thick wheels of his Triumph. Downstairs
cats purr under an afghan, noses like the
slotted heat vents in our old Plymouth Fury.

Frozen limbs scrape against the Sears
aluminum. I can't not think about yesterday,
third period, my oldest crush calling my long nose
"Scandinavian," leaning into my ear as he whispered
I should meet him tomorrow after the bell.

Now the snow sheds as if a great white dog
shakes awake from his afternoon nap.
Salt trucks lumber past. I think of getting
some tea from the kitchen, but the bed
offers a more thorough kind of warmth,

the windows offer a clear view of this powder
that has stopped time. I'm sure that my mother
felt this—in a bedroom in her hometown, in a climate
much colder and more prone to complications,
about a man less handsome, more timid than my father.

And now she is nowhere. When the phone rings
just imagine all of life's small disasters.

The Same River Twice

Mornings, we like to kiss then pour coffee.
When we met, he was studying fluvial

geomorphology—the way rivers transport
sediments. He tied flies under a hot halo of light.

When we hiked he explained rock formations.
Now there are several things besides love.

Two dogs who curl on couches with ears
fanned out like chenille throws. A city

full of climate-change deniers. Evenings,
it takes several hours reading in chairs

for us to feel human. We fall asleep at 8 p.m.
Mornings, we like to kiss then pour coffee.

Cottonwood Long Shot

Last night's high-country rain has riveted the dirt,
frosted the trailhead with peaks and valleys of cake-y soil.

Tufts and clumps mud the ground between the pinions,
prickly pears, juniper and oak. We stare down the 2000

feet left to drop; world stained with layers of red and green
so profound we joke they won't wash off. The morning wind

finds our ears, and the sun becomes us: something sustaining.
To hike into a canyon takes a special kind of faith.

Today, we trust that the long shot's sweeping contours will
lead us to nature's close-up. Soon we will see not this solid

ribbon of green, but one cottonwood, one sycamore, one alder.
Otherwise, why go? Beauty lives here too.

We trust the path, and see from the top the riparian
lips that will swallow our measured steps.

We see shades and curves,
the earth's wrinkled throat.

Goodbye, Ohio

I think this is what I know:
corn in moronic rows. A few
cows lisping near the barn.

Father in the house cleaning a dish.
Mother cozy in her latest asylum.
Ragweed descends like snow.

Crops on the brain,
father sends me to mice the fields,
his low-ground cat-lover child.

I find no mice skimming the dirt.
I find no cicadas, no starlings.
The sun will come careening

through the kitchen window.
And I will bolt west for
my own feline sky.

Mia

Today she is a goddess whose
third eye is a blind bruise.
Small children aren't my gig. But

here at the cabin, the lake
where I spent summers before
the family went nuclear, I can't

keep my eyes off Mia, the blond
totterer, who could have risen
from a photo of me at two,

life-preservered, bending
at the shore to agate-search, pointing
tiny fingers towards a mid-lake loon.

And in some struggling language
she asks me: to take her *simming*, to *hode*
her hand, like the cat who sits

on the lap of the sneezer, out of
cousin after cousin in a land of breeders
she chooses me to walk her into the water

where she won't swim, but won't
go back to land. And that's how I end up
with a baby. The woman most vocally

childfree. For a moment with Mia on my hip
I think if only I had procreated maybe
my parents would not have gone

insane. That they would have loved
seeing me adore my lakeside children,
the way they adored me before I hit

puberty. Maybe we would have
stopped fighting each other,
turned our attention to baby.

We would hold her when she's *seepy*, watch
her swing in the hammock, catch her before
she falls, before her forehead kisses rock.

Remission

Pigeons nest in the front palms
song clocking the afternoon
their white rain storming.

Birds remind us who was first on this earth.
The universe dares us to touch anything.
Yesterday we walked your boyhood streets

overgrown with oaks, watched your father
filling just enough space to not be gone,
tossed rocks into the Severn river,

took the 10 a.m. flight back to Phoenix.
Today when I enter the car my earrings blaze,
burn my neck when I turn my head to back

out of my parking space. Some people
are longer for this world than others.
I want to hold them in my hands like a bird.

Tornado Hijinks

Twisters love April in Ohio. Mom
yanked me by my fine blond hair.

That's a lie. She was never violent.
I just don't want to think of her

face in that moment. The window
rattle accelerating like a kettle,

the pitchy whistle as I stared
into the backyard and refused

to join her at the basement stairs.
I was only three years old! And oh

the watering can flying over
the rose bush, whitecap waves

in the deep end of the pool. I'll never forget
her plaintive call: *daughter, daughter*!

Golden Dragon, Takeout

Chinese food when
our kitchen brims
with fresh tomatoes,
peppers, squash.

Here's the Kung Pao.
Your father is dying.
I have no idea what to do
except feed you.

I arrange the plate while
you call for flights.
You're so quiet it feels like
I'm losing you both.

Between our four parents
there isn't one good lung.
Soon there will be six out of
eight lungs to wheeze.

Underneath the Tamaracks

My mother in a circle of light
in the kitchen tracing a coffee
ring at the round oak table
her mouth pierced like O
to blow slow smoke,
her red bikini slipping,
the stunning color contrast of
public vs. private skin.

Age eleven, my most exotic visions
are in grocery store checkouts:
the backs of young women.
Bumpy straps beneath cotton shirts.
My own chest is tender,
nipples fat and pointed,
protruding like small candies.

A trip to teacher's farm.
We meet her lover, a small woman.
She helps us mount the horses
on a back acre near the barn.

It's a great leisure
knowing just where to put one's self.
Age eleven my body fits places:
three steps in each concrete slab
on the sidewalk to school,
underneath the tamaracks,
inside the large Allen urn.

How miniature, how clean
it must seem to my father,
viewing us from an airplane window.

Return flight from
Amsterdam, Rio, Caracas.
Circling his city, his neighborhood,
his little family.
Plummeting towards
this perfect summary.

Beeturia

They were bulbous. I chose the biggest ones.
Stalks draped over the cart's edge.

You picked proteins while I picked produce.
We would meet up again in dairy.

When you approached, I pulled the beets from the cart
to show off, as if this were my own harvest.

At home while you grilled, I mixed the greens with garlic,
some olive oil in the pan. Then I peeled and chopped these

beets the size of oranges, cupping chunks with blood-red palms.
We chewed. Then smiled at each other with rubies for teeth.

Overnight we each peed in the dark, so this morning when
the bowl looked like your father's catheter-bag after chemo,

we downed water, waiting to see who peed lemonade;
who peed iced tea. Yours was bright red, as if you were

cut through. And though later we learned it was harmless,
we spent the morning showing each other more than our

usual kindness, flashing forward to our own deaths:
how they will start with a noticeable change in shade.

Aravaipa Canyon

Walls tower. The squeezed
water rushes. Coatimundi

click up cliffs, their ringed
tails bouncing. After five miles

we set up camp between mouths,
kiss under cottonwoods. It's three-ish,

the desert's highest hour.
One lone yellow warbler.

Then, such whooping!
We scramble through

alders and willows to see
one smallish swim hole,

two boys, two men, whose
pistols in hike-holsters

suggest they might shoot
mountain lion, black bear,

bighorn sheep, or tent thief?
We hesitate, they whoop.

Jim Beam in flasks.
Burning skin. Paunches.

Then their skinny arms wave,
point to one high overhang.

They cajole. So we climb.
Check for loach minnows.

We jump. Splashing through
the dark green algae of delight.

Dying, Four Ways: Maryland

Take your boat down to the Severn, drop

your crab pots. Ignore the cough and keep

smoking. Let the Cocker Spaniel pee

on the carpet. Try radiation, drink protein

shakes and Ensure. Have a lung out. Flatline

in the operating room, but fight your way back

so you can have ten more months, during which

you will drive your Jeep up the street to Aloupis's

for Budweisers. Watch one more Orioles season.

Olive Warbler Whip Pan

It's a steep grade, not steady, cut through towering cliffs
and sloping rock. A hawk throws his shadow to the ground.

It's always this way, descending. Buckling knees from dry to lush.
Each texture leaves its mark: wind turns warm, sun reddens,

sandstone benches beckon. We stop to eat apples. We watch
a group of uniformed boy scouts hut into a single file line.

And before long we'll also be rewarded with dark pools and falls.
The globe's glue, the sedimentary tumble of the earth. Wait.

What's that? Olive warbler? Painted orangestart? Scissor-tailed
flycatcher? Some pied piper sings so we know we must soon start.

Is it due to our dread of moving that we suddenly hear them sing?
All of my life I have not loved the plaintive calls of birds,

but in the underbrush we hear the Dean Martin of mourning doves,
Oh-we-oh-wooh-wooh. And his voice will spur us down the canyon,

the 1000 feet left to drop. It would be easier with wings
to soar over alligator juniper, manzanita, yucca. It's hard

work hiking, and we promise if we get home
we will learn all there is to know about birds.

Good Fences

She shushes her dogs in high-pitched staccato pulses,
slams between laundry and hamhock.

The fragrance excites more barking. She tortillas
the beans. Each morning she reminds her boy

that at his age she and her siblings
stole eggs from behind the carnecería,

went to school dirty if at all, played *fight*
with her uncles as the noon got drunker.

Her boy once tossed his keys into my pool.
Timid, he mumbled the physics of falling

on the wrong side of the world.
He fears my white bleating of cats

since his is a life of dogs.
She and I are more alike than different.

Fifty feet between our bodies on this earth.
All day we await our men. We rearrange dishware.

Each afternoon we do the trimming, pony-tailed.
We read in a soft chair as a good excuse to nap.

Ross Township Feed and Tackle

My horse was *Pronto,* yours just *Red,*
and though the air was thirty degrees cooler than
it would be at lunch, we brushed them down,
the light fog lifting, their noses more intimate
than we could understand at twelve.

Later, riding through a rocky stretch, one
behind us spooked, reared, the girl atop him
screaming, her neocolonial house near Cleveland,
her liver and white pointer, all flashing
before her in a pre-teen moment when

life is as intangible as our own tender breast-skin.
So we stopped to eat ham sandwiches, spray extra
Off, the humidity weighing down our cotton shorts,
frizzing our hair. I have known you for as long
as I have known. Last year they closed

our camp, settled a class action suit against
the "Feed and Tackle" two miles away, which was
really Fernald Uranium processing plant, with its own
barn and silo, so no one asked. Four girls like us, "vets,"
proud of our five-summer runs were diagnosed:

gave way to the infiltrating illnesses, cursed the perky
campfire songs, the weeks away from carpeted homes,
put the settlements in Trusts. So you are pregnant.
Your parents will get their sixth grandchild
while mine wait for the mail in slippers, mumbling

over stale coffee and last week's paper, shuffling
out to the box then back in again. You are still
in Ohio. I am in a perpetual

bad mood. No one
wants to ride anymore, light a fire, hike
to the watertower.

Dog-Eared

With sharp scissors he snipped
their silky ears. Sent the tips falling

like leaves leaving our beautiful dogs.
Ears I have kissed, caressed more

than I have him lately, the doe-y hair
on his forearms that made me fall in love.

I picked up the parts. Thought about
stitches, several, that could make

the ears soft again, smooth, pat-
worthy; I obsessed over nerves, veins.

Would blood flow back? Would rust coats
grow again? But the ears were already dry,

flaky as rawhides. We had been fighting and
he cut their ears to punish me. My perfect,

literal companions. Who know no sarcasm.
Who show their care in wiggles. He cut

their ears off. I woke knowing
I would never forgive him.

Velvet Ash Cross-Cut

Finally on a flat, the relentless slope has straightened, but we still tilt
as if disembarking from a leaning ship. The new constant is the roar,

20,000 gallons an hour, and the sun's heat off the rocks.
It's the symbiosis we came for: the cold water, the hot stone.

When the trail levels and forks we follow the sound
of the falls like two charmed snakes. The floodplain

surprises, awash with verdant underbrush. Pines and spines
give way to leaves and grasses. We know we're closing in

when we see our first evidence of water: a sopping terrier,
drenched and wiry. He shakes off some drops, leads us

down the last steps like some doggy harbinger of water,
some furry wander-lusting mutt. We blink once and he's gone.

We're alone in a stand of velvet ash, wind in the leaves
tinkling like the world's most delicate chimes.

Did we dream it? Terrier, velvet ash.
Velvet ash, terrier? Then we hear the bark.

We meander around the bend, see for certain the soggy terrier,
wave to his man and woman, bless the water and its banks.

Plucked

Creosote, why are you looking at me

    like I'm the one with a bunny under

my yellow skirt? All you need to do is

    stink when wet. Grow, grow, grow

with next to no encouragement.

    Like mother on the psych ward,

rearranging her bed-stand so that all items

    are perfectly arms-length.

Ohio morning, Ohio afternoon.

    The things that wake us

do not have to be frightening.

    My god. How did she un-earth

all the intricate trills?

    Would they fit into my harvest basket?

Since later I'd board a plane

    for a different desert.

Finding a Center

On this morning's ride
I heard a siren behind me.

A mile down I saw flashing lights,
a car facing east on a west-bound curb.

The downed biker's feet were still stuck
in his pedals like the world was on its side.

When I told my father
why it upset me, he described

the time in the Philippines when
he rode a motorcycle into the jungle.

It was muddy. He slid several feet.
The bike landed on his good leg.

My father's polio left no muscles
from his right knee down.

Once at a wedding a girl asked me
why he limped. I was thirteen, the age

when children learn their parents
are conspiring to disappoint them.

A hot air balloon lifted like a head.
I turned to her, honestly. *He limps?*

This morning I only wanted
comforting. I repeated, it was

my very route. He answered
he was sorry it scared me.

He said he used to wish
he could ride a bike.

But his left foot was always
chasing the pedal,

his right foot always
dragging on the ground.

Past Black Canyon City

White-knuckling the climb up I-17,
we can't help but argue about safe

driving, the ramshackle trucks
with trailers hogging what back east

we call the "speed lane." Lines of late
models are stuck behind semis

the entire 100-mile, 6000-foot climb.
Only the tempers here are quick.

Past Black Canyon City a truck
burns in the median. The bulbous

flames shimmer. A thin man, young, waits
close enough to suggest suicide or idiocy.

Traffic slows from dense curiosity,
is quickly forgotten come sharp grade,

Winnebago, watch for falling rocks, divided
highway separating your will from mine.

Blue Juice Sky

Stalled, wing-deep in road-kill, the vulture
stares towards our rushing, flicks away
just as our tires straddle another anonymous carcass.
The bird jerks skyward, his beak packed with flesh, bone.

At the trailhead our doors open, our cold air meets hot.
Temperatures converge and compete for all the dark
pockets of my body. We discuss what won't fit
into my pack: cook stove, white fuel, tent and pads,

a bladder of wine. I am softer. We know my lungs will
cramp and fill, offering fluid like a pot of strained peas.
The sun is you: everywhere. In moments my skin is moist.
My eyes pound and film. Rock and dirt shimmer like light.

Three hours deep we startle a pack of coatimundi. As each
disappears over the ridge I remember my neighbor in and out
of sight on his roof, his a/c whining with some inefficacy,
his wife at the window, bare breast exposed, the baby clawing
like a soft red lizard. I can't decide when to care for you. Or how.

Eschew

I've realized too late it's not children

I dislike, it's parents. So I stay alone

with the only three things I own:

a knit cap, a felt pen, a glass pitcher

with a long crack near the handle.

How I love the heft of my negative

net worth! I can tell what

day of the week it is by

counting the bananas.

Dying, Four Ways: Arizona

Lose your husband of fifty years while you

go blind. Leave the Bay for the Desert.

Complain about Bush/Cheney and eat

sandwiches while watching CNN. Flirt with

the paramedics. Tell everyone you have quit,

then sneak smokes all day. Buy identical

Tencel suits in three colors that you will never wear

because we're not going to go to Charleston's

for ribs anymore. No Olive Garden, no lasagna.

Rantasies

Alamos Mexico, November 2007

Like chainsaws slicing the fronds
of Mexican fan palms at 2 a.m.
Like leaf blowers fueling

mini tornadoes in cobbled streets.
Even here in the Sierra Madre foothills,
bougainvillea circling a tiled pool,

just months after we heard the whistle
of your mother's last breath,
I startle from the deepest slumber

my mind making lists of grievances
I'll never have the nerve to deliver
to her family who abandoned her

because they were too busy breeding.
You love me, it is true. But now I am
the Pointer in dream. You see the twitch,

twitch of eyelids, the palsied paws,
my white hot want of rabbit.
Now even the Fiesta of Nuestra Señora

can't expunge these rants. Right outside
our hacienda, pilgrims crawl on their knees
to make their mandas to the Virgin.

Their bells clang well before dawn. But by then
I have already stirred: brain-shouting, bruxing.
Like horses rearing on hind legs. Like pirámides

made of children: three chubby boys, then two
thin girls. Then on top, the earth's skinniest
fledgling. Wobbling, she raises her pale arms high.

South Mountain Park

When we moved to the mountain I expected

javelina eating the rhododendrons, knocking

over trash cans. I imagined the park as an ocean.

Our "waterfront" property: sea of creosote, saguaro.

But every day the cars commence their rushing.

City trucks, delivery vans, SUVs, sedans,

backhoes, RVs, and motorcycles.

In the park I pretend I am a boat dipping, rolling

away from homes and roads and anything

produced or sold. But back at our lot the traffic

is spilling, surging, dumping:

the black Lexus, the blue minivan,

the yellow bus.

Returning to a Place Known Only in Childhood

My grandfather's house
is tearing itself down.
The buckeyes and sweet
williams have spread
and canary grass covers
the railway where
as children we rushed
to feel the tracks,
warm after the trains passed.
The old neighbor's fields
are smaller than I remember.
So is the rented shack near the station
where my grandfather
and his father before him
came to drink bourbon
between seventeen-hour shifts.
Most men in my family
worked the Ohio rails.
But I know my father
by his contrails, by
the occasional thunder
of engines as he slows to land.
A bluebird flies overhead,
its wings clapping,
reminding me
the thing wasted is not my life
nor the summers spent,
snap bean and corn husk.

Impingement

I asked the PT assistant, *What is the most*
painful thing that ever happened to you?
as he squirted cold gel on my injured shoulder.
He was Greek. Italian maybe. With black
eyelashes so long he might have swept the floor
by blinking. Half my age. He thought about it

as he drew a figure eight on my pale skin.
I broke my wrist once. I was ten. So I pictured
his young Italian or Greek mother, with dark
hair on her arms, picking up her broken son
and feeling broken herself. *But it only hurt*
for a moment, he said, not as an apology,

(I was going on three months of thrice-weekly visits)
but as an acknowledgment of soft tissue versus bone,
of the tears I could never quite manage to hold back.
My blue eyes met his. And what do I know
of brown? It's all new to me. Daily spasms.
I can't even take off a shirt or put dishes on a shelf.

I had a cast, he said. And he searched the ceiling so I knew
he was remembering the drive to the doctor's, his classmates
signing the plaster. And he continued talking, though
I had moved on to thinking it would be a fun joke to ask
what the wand saw, *is it a boy or a girl?* He was young enough
to be my son. Had I had one. Had I had a son with brown eyes.

Salome

How does a man
breeze into this
canyon with only
a pocketful of
nuts. Plaid
coat, walking stick.
Handkerchiefing
forehead. Sniffly
dog furring
pounding descent
into the canyon.
Foot sweat, backache.
He claims trout,
stream fed, catches them
two at a time. He will
wander down to not
disturb us. Calls
dog breath dripping tongue
mid-drink. They are
tail flash, disappearing
trail. We are
warm camp stove, fettuccine,
Bushmills flask,
sleeping bag, camp chair,
water filter, coffee mug,
kiss me. We are
ten miles deep
into the gash.

Day Trip, Guadalupe Mercado

Blowing off work, five women
come to get strawberries, serapes,
Talavera pots. As soon as we cross
Baseline the Priest Drive signs
change to Avenida del Yaqui.
We park at the *Bienvenidos* mural—
cooing the crank of roasting chilies
in their barrel, corn on its cob.
Our server explains the camarones
al ajillo is her grandmother's recipe.
We nod, downing our Dos Equis.
Later we buy piñatas, hammered
copper mirrors, mangoes, pears.
Picking our fruit more carefully than Eve.

Three Pound Cutthroat

We came a long way
up this mountain for trout.

At dawn our metal lures pierce
the sheer surface of the water.

By noon I want to catch anything:
crawdad, dragonfly, you.

Below at 1,000 feet the century plants
commence their suicide blooming.

There is just enough energy
to reproduce and die.

When you catch it I am
in the woods, impatient.

I return to find the severed head,
the gills still flapping like wings.

Dusk is slow, the fish slower.
Thick flesh spastic in the pan.

I want you to kiss me,
but here are all the stars.

The stars and the spaces between stars
it has taken me all my life to accept.

Sycamore Close-Up

We continue downstream, grateful for the water's rush,
the shaded passage. Not far in we meet a group of fallen

trees with trunks as wide as kayaks. One shoots its roots upward,
a large hand waving from the depths of the earth. So how did they fall?

Rushing water? Wind? A mule deer's tender summer antlers?
One downed tree crosses the stream bed: bridge for sale!

A pair of trees make a shady creek gazebo. Like matchsticks,
the others lean against each other, ripe for flame.

Despite the trees' strange demeanor, each trunk wears its spots
like barky macramé, some clustering of color surely crafted

by arbory artisans. Close-up, the bark reveals itself
in jigsaw puzzle pieces of gray and green.

Then today's pattern presents itself. We see minnows in a pool
seeking insects, their delicate mouths leaving concentric rings.

Everywhere we look there are circles: round wisps of cloud
as if the gods were blowing smoke, a layer of oxidized granite

ringing the cliff walls, a flock of turkey vultures circling a kill,
halos of lichen crowning the rock: an alliance

between two kingdoms: fungus and algae, a partnership
without soil, shimmering like a blissful spill.

Little Colorado

Sky feigning interest.
Yesterday when she called
I was dreaming bakeries:
tall baguettes, organic boules.
Now in the river there is water.
Desert shimmering under a weight
I might never comprehend.
I look at her face in a photo,
teeth white like bones.
Can I see her future there?
Can I find the crack
that turns to crevasse?
How did I save my mother
from suicide? When I can't even
land a trout in a stocked stream.

Studious

for Phil Longo

Umbrellas dot the beach like nylon stars.
Last year MTV crews lined the Boulevard.
This year a toddler on a ladybug beach towel
eats a sandwich. Her mother toes the water,
stares at the pontoons overflowing with frat boys.

In class you were soft-spoken, a Phillies fan,
your goal to be a US Marshall. You were
handsome. One classmate confided her crush.
Later she couldn't stop imagining your body
limp in the lake where she learned to swim.

Was that you, rising from the waves?
Muttering apologies for your tardiness,
your homework dripping and smeared.
I see the churning water, the hot bow
of the boat, your green eyes wide with

the slow vertigo of gravity, the abbreviated
silence of your fall. I hear the boys slurring
against the splash and suck, pecking around
the boat, clumsy against the rocking, each
wondering why this moment has chosen to be
so different from the one just before it, a game.

Like older brother in the deep end, legs
pumping against the cold, suburban lung
of water. He always resurfaced, laughing.
But you stayed under for months
as if there was something to learn.

My 3 a.m. Problem

Not insomnial, but on the edge
of sleep, I compose in that moment
between dog bark and cat vomit
the poem that I've been trying to write
since writing started. But not to wake you
I stay in bed and beg my memory to work
where it has always failed.

So this morning I'm grasping fragments
of burnt toast that is something, a water tower
that is a cupcake, and how I wanted to tell you that
loving you is a Pyrex bowl and a wooden spoon.

Sprawl

My five a.m. run catapults me from sheets to streets.

The sky seems to have suffered a pink spill.

The neighbors are baking like loaves in their oven-beds.

Their cars have been breeding again.

By six a.m. front doors are opening like skin flaps.

Robed men leaning one-armed for their papers.

I stride past houses so much like my own

my mind won't stop asserting our differences.

Beauty Salon: Tempe, Arizona

David lingers on my earlobes
after a lavender scalp massage.
Every fifth Friday for fifteen years,
he smiles at me in the mirror as he
trims my sun-dried ends. In college
he studied geography, started a Master's
before his marriage. He begs for details
about our latest hike. I talk and he nods,
yes, yes—he has lived in this desert
his lifetime. Has seen kids like me
come and go. Has driven his VW
in Box Canyon before the dirt-bikes,
before the ATVs with rifle racks,
before the RVs and SUVs. Young,
yes, but I too have seen the pink-tiled
fingers groping all the soft crotches
of this desert. I ask, what will be left for
his daughter, then some day her daughter,
the earth's young heir? David smiles
at my sweet concern. He flicks the smock
like a muleta. We watch the flaxen snips
fall like bull hair to the ground.

Obligatorium

You don't have to floss all your teeth!
Only the ones you want to keep.
                    —Dr Dacey, DDS, Cincinnati, Ohio

It was before latex gloves, before dentists stopped
giving lollipops to good little patients. We all had

so many teeth, just as we had so many arms
and so many legs. And what could stop us

from playing kick-the-can three more times
before our mothers' voices grew hoarse? It was

the seventies. Everything was avocado, gold, or
corduroy. We played doctor in the basement,

while our parents watched M*A*S*H through the haze
of Benson & Hedges, sipping Glenfiddich out of Waterfords.

Now I think I should go back to my grade school, squeeze
my fat ass into a tiny blue chair, tell those ponytails

and huskies to demand candy from the dentist, to steal
the key to the liquor cabinet, to loiter on the block until

after dark, until after their parents make good on their
promises, until they flossed the last great tooth of the earth.

Dying, Four Ways: Nevada

Wake up and make a pot of coffee. Take a

no-doze or three. Read an article from *Harper's*

while chewing Nicorette. Adjust your

cannula and turn off NPR. Walk back towards

your home office to start work for the day.

Clutch your chest, trip over the laundry

basket, and land facedown so that the blood

pools into your face like a bruise so bad

the coroner demands a closed casket.

Pinetop Lakeside

Near the Little Colorado
a woman's brown hair
changes quietly to blond,
her legs sting with nettles,
the path of her childhood
teems with chokeberries.
Later she will pick peaches,
boil them in a pot until
the fuzz undresses itself
exposing the brains of the tree.
She portioned her acres into
lots. New owners drive up,
build their cabins from kits.
Now she soaks in the tub,
counting the squares of tile
like the tiles of land
her mother and father
owned. In the kitchen
the chutney rattles its lid.
The trowel and the fork,
could be dangerous, says her son.
He has accepted the duty
of worrying about edges
while she worries about
the bright validity of sunshine,
the dog's water, the blackbird.
And when her son
insists, she packs
a picture, some books,
her grandmother's letters
and settles in the city, where
there is room for her
since most everyone else
has left.

Hualapai Hilltop

From the trailhead we zig
and zag a full mile down.

We pass burros nodding up,
loaded down with rucksacks

owned by bodies cool in the bellies
of choppers overhead.

Waterfalls await us, deep
travertine pools. Blues

and greens brilliant as a
bird. In ten miles we'll

drop three thousand feet,
through the town of Supai,

we'll wonder which horses
hoofed in the mattresses, bikes,

fence posts and the café's
cash register. Now here

are the troops weary with sweat,
some so weak they must be

flown to their barracks, over the
tamarisk and into a bed of sand.

Tents dot the landscape.
We feel the prop, prop of engines,

stop at a make-shift station,
obtain a pass. Inch our way

into the territory, approach the
indelible beauty of the front line.

A Frog's Courage

Then it is time to spread her ashes. There are

flight delays, torrential rain, a minor tornado.

It's hard to say where the frogs are going.

From one lake to a better lake?

But this is porous country.

What else hasn't mother told me?

I've been driving miles, and still

the squish under the tires.

Her ashes belted

in the back seat

like a baby.

Losing Track of Daylight

Hawks hang as if suspended by strings.
The wind is violent. Pond water launches

its assembly line of slapping.
At 9,000 feet the air is more

present than less. Motor homes dot
the state highway. We find our favorite

spot, a sliver of BLM land between two
ranches, our tent on a slight downward

slope, our sleeping bags zipped into one.
You seduce me this way since it smells

like Ohio, pine trees, a threatening storm,
cows munching past as if to warn of rain.

They bow necks in a tight avalanche
of chewing, move where the others

move, drink when there is thirst,
bat the great eyelash of the womb.

Charity

I dearly loved that Great Aunt we all had,
Catholic, nearly a nun, named Sis, who smashed

parsnips and made our fathers stomach
them without butter. Who read our poetry

and said women should quit complaining.
Who took us shopping for school clothes,

disliked denim; fingered only houndstooth.
Who never married but who scathed

about poorly matched unions, ill-advised
pregnancies. Who surprised us all by leaving

more money than Jesus, mostly to churches.
Who slighted certain nieces for reasons nobody

could fathom. Whose lawyers took years
to track down every random beneficiary.

I like to think of her writing that will.
Nearly blind from glaucoma. Fingers

knotted like green beans. Rifling
through the files of everyone else's

failures as she contemplated kneeling
before her own forgiving God.

What Good Does a Drop Do

Burn line runs the length
of the mountain spine.
I could comb your hair
with the tree teeth of the ridge.

Red-tailed hawks
circle the smolder-wind,
insidious in this,
their own slow dying.

At our cabin I left a watering can
months before the blazes,
not in any way for watering,
but as a hint of leisure.

As if we have time to
garden or know how.
It is easy to be pious when
your life is not on fire.

Here ours is a life of lanterns,
wood stoves, chairs worn on the arms.
And so what if the wind stopped the fire
an acre away from our own rustic wood?

Ashes coat nightstands as far away as Phoenix,
traveling those miles to warn:
watering can, birch tree,
insistence of the flame.

Day Trip, Cave Creek Guided Tours

Tightening the reins only
propels our horses faster.
Cholla clumping at the ankle.
The *Trail Boss Adventure Package*
takes us two hours deep into
the Majestic Sonoran Desert,
includes *Authentic Cowboy Games*,
a *Classic Cowboy Lunch*, is capped
at eight. We are five women breaking
the monotony of mid-careers,
three portly men in from Denver,
all saddle-sore and getting burned.
Our wrangler explains this route was
used by stagecoaches travelling
between Phoenix and Flagstaff.
Past the fire pit we drop into slough.
Reeds slap jeans, cottonwoods
brush foreheads. Cameras flash
like strobe lights from the banks.
Our *wonderfully conditioned*
and *well-mannered* horses nod
across state trust land, their noses
quietly suffering our pats of bully love.

Dying, Four Ways: Ohio

Answer every phone call without fail. Lie

and say you went to the grocery store

for beans and metts. Lose 100 pounds. Let

a tumor grow so large you're blind in one eye.

Pretend you have a bad cold. At the hospital,

ask to be patched up and sent home. Give those

who love you five days to say goodbye. When I say,

"This is Jill. She has come to write the will."

You say, "My name is Ed and I can be misled."

Chiricahuas

Sky islands rise from a grassland sea.
We climb their rock spires: ash layers

erupted by the Turkey Creek Volcano
27 million years before our parents

ever dreamed of disappointing us.
We approach a steep ridge, watch clouds

sink. We suck what used to be anger
into our lungs. They might never mend.

From here to there is not impossible.
It is only a chant, a stream, a crossing.

Buckeye

Your spotted head cold. Mouth bloody.
Two hours ago I left in a huff.
I had given up trying to catch you.
You wouldn't leave that gecko on the fence.
My anger at you heaved like a last breath.

When I came home I called your name.
I searched the wall where you had hunted.
Checked both gates fearing that your nose had
led you beyond the yard you loved. Didn't think
to stare into the still prism of the deep end.

When I pulled you limp and dripping from the pool
your one speckled ear flopped open, revealing
a new pink universe. I blew into your muzzle,
pounded your freckled chest. And in death
you behaved much as you did in life.

Now when I hear your jingle all that appears
is the ghost of you. When I sleep, your name is
a puff of smoke in the searing air. My mind sweats,
its beads forming crystals on the pillow.
I pull them like rubies from my long blond hair.

Punkin Center Lodge and Liquor

The twinning of the state route scalpeled seven ranches,
incision sealed with asphalt. Like tripping on stairs,

a man remembers driving his grandfather's tractor.
Jukebox wailing Hank Williams draws him inside.

Men wear their sun damage like saris, smoke Camels.
When Toyotas pull in, late models with bike racks,

men shift on stools, crane necks to catch glimpses of the girls
coming from the swim hole in Gisela. Coeds from state schools

their parents argued weren't academic enough. They smile
at the tired ranchers, mouthing made-up words to the music.

He stares at the one with her head tilted back, her torso
bronzed. He imagines her as a child, flying down the Beeline

in the back of her parent's minivan, collecting license plates
to beat her brother, pulling Cokes from the cooler,

reading Nancy Drews and staring out the window at him,
the ranch, and his grandfather coughing under his wide brim.

Tell Your Story Walking

What's madness but nobility of soul
At odds with circumstance?
—Theodore Roethke

Every morning I stay in bed until I get my waking bearings.

I have a dog at my feet, and a dog just at the tip of my fingers.

Getting up makes me feel like a good girl.

I go downstairs and drink a liter of water and two cups of coffee.

I read the paper while eating two poached eggs and fruit.

Then I spend the morning terrified about what I am going to do next.

I was fifteen when you went mad.

I got scarlet fever.

With my babysitting money, I bought a car you hated but dad loved.

You stopped eating or sleeping.

You wanted something from me that felt like a foreign language.

Now I'm stuck here making such delicate choices.

Upon waking, I can pet the dog or the other dog.

Before you died you called and said, *I have wanted to say something.*

I said, *Okay.*

You said, *Sweetie, I did the best I could.*

There are two ways to tell a story.

When I was fifteen you went mad and I saved you.

When I was fifteen you went mad and I never forgave you.

How to Make a Lake

At two and a half I escaped the crib,
wandered downstairs to the crimson

décolletage of home-grown tomatoes in
a basket, I clutched those orbs in my hands,

watched the tender skin split into so many
wide crevasses, the thousand eyes of heaven.

Years later, on the Ohio, I woke to watch
crews trussing the Taylor-Southgate bridge.

I watched the sluggishness of steel and concrete,
the stone slow process of crossing. All night

I saw the glowing torch and broad shoulders
of a man who waved from his platform-raft.

I miss tomatoes in July, dried leaves in October.
Now they are building a lake in the Sonoran.

Planting inflatable barricades in the riverbed,
canals flushing water from the Colorado.

At night I feel the lake filling, rising, so that when
I bleed the east squeezes my womb like a lemon.

Mid-Street

I trace your veins
like routes on a map to
someone else's silence.

Not to ours, not to the
houses on separate rivers
where we learned this:

thick smoke clears
chimneys of robins,
orioles, cardinals.

My first kiss was
different from my
first kiss with you.

We were greedy.
The car glowed,
its wings wide open.

Now I want it back.
I want you to deliver it
to me, surprise the small

spaces where I store
delight, the small spaces
where birds hide.

Go Anywhere

A Phoenix park ranger discovered a petroglyph
had been excised. She followed the trail rut
to the McMansion of a man who answered
his door dressed in a towel, the stolen rock
well-lit above his mantel. And what is there

to say? I'm certain there are topics about which
I know nothing. I moved from Ohio to this desert
with two suitcases and a poorly laid plan. The first
week I was here I called the landlord to complain
about dust and he explained monsoons to me.
I'm still bitching my way through triple digits.

If you could go anywhere, where would you go?
You and I can, now that all four of our parents died.
I thought I'd move to France, maybe lose too much
weight. But I fell in love with you and here we are.
So now what? Will we go to the Costco, maybe Home

Depot? I don't know. I don't know if we'll have time.
Should we go to the park, help ourselves to free wall art?
Since living here already feels like stealing?

Wednesday's Path

It is what we all want:
tight curl of the leaf,

monumental shadow
of the storm.

From this high cliff
the surfers are flailing gulls.

You have asked for my
forgiveness. Below, the waves

pound their white drums.
Time to remember

the meticulous accounting
of daughters. Those

bright, sharp edges
on the periphery of praise.

Fossil Springs Cutaway

It's a problem with canyons: what goes down must
come up. Figure double the time it takes to descend.

We point our noses at the trail and march.
The bottom drops out as we head for the deep blue sky.

The air cools, but skin warms. We hear our hearts
instead of wind in our ears. We're surprised

by a group hiking down with no packs.
The sun is dropping as quickly as they are.

Back at the trailhead the cars have multiplied.
We read their many stickers: Be Green,

Fur is for Animals, Wake up and Smell the Fascism.
Soon someone's playing a car stereo, honking a horn.

We need to close our eyes, take a breath.
Then we drive down the Beeline, drop

4500 feet in ninety miles. Back to pile-ups
on the I-10, ninety-five-degree low temps, jobs,

husbands, pets to feed, laundry to wash.
But we'll always have this on film:

the cottonwood, the sycamore,
the lichen and the dove.

Turning Forty

I am a tall

canyon from which

water has dried.

I am a tall

stand of alders.

I am the first

bird on new wings.

Under the weight

of these stars a

new type of tea

steeps in my bones.

June

is already unraveling like the loose

thread the cat bats. I thought I could

plan the next forty years based on my

forty years' experience. Why is living

still so problematic? The days slip

away as quickly as memories

of a person who was like me.

Now I am stuck re-learning

that all pain is public. I want to listen

to it over the phone so it sounds skinny.

I want it to be the dentist whose sleeve

brushes the curve of my cheekbone.

I don't want to hate it as much as I do.

I need to tell you that last thing I said

was insincere.

About the Cover Artist

Bedelgeuse is an anatomical collage artist. Work created under the Bedelgeuse alias includes cut paper collage, digital collage, and mixed media sculptural collage all centered around human anatomy. Source material used comes from old science and medical books that are in the public domain. Artwork are both physical cut-paper and digital collages that form into a wild amalgamation of botanical, zoological, and anatomical imagery. These compositions produce synergetic visuals that represent humanity's inherent relationship to nature and the universe.

Bedelgeuse currently resides in San Francisco, California, and has received no formal visual arts education.

Bedelgeuse has had artwork in numerous group and solo exhibitions worldwide including Tokyo, New York, San Francisco, Rio De Janeiro, and London. He has upcoming installations and exhibitions in various cities worldwide. Bedelgeuse has also had multiple features in various magazines and social media including Instagram, Tumblr, Juxtapoz, Hi Fructose, and many independent publications.